GLORIOUS
FRUIT
DESSERTS

Consulting Editor:
Valerie Ferguson

southwater

Contents

Introduction

There is something special about the first strawberries of the summer and the first crisp apples of the autumn. While supermarkets provide an astonishing array of fresh fruit all year round, nothing tastes quite so wonderful or succulent as newly ripened fruits in season.

Raw fruit is the perfect snack, and nutritionists recommend eating several portions each day. However, to discover its full glory it is worth spending a little time making a special dessert. Some, such as fresh fruit salads, can be ready in minutes. Others, such as sorbets and ice creams, take little time to prepare but do require time for freezing. Pies and tarts can be as elaborate or as simple as you want them to be, and fruit also offers the cook an opportunity to make imaginative desserts for entertaining.

Fruit is immensely versatile; it is delicious served hot or cold and combines superbly with many other ingredients.

You are sure to find the ideal recipe for a fruit-based dessert in this book, whether for a family supper, an informal lunch with friends or a sophisticated dinner party. Don't forget that recipes can often be varied using fruits in season—so enjoy the luscious flavors of fruit all year round.

Types of Fruit

The range of fruits available has never been so extensive, and new varieties are appearing all the time.

Apples & Pears

The most popular of all fruits, apples are perfect for eating raw or in hot or cold desserts and are available all year round. There are many flavors and textures to choose from.

Apples

Sweet and juicy pears have fine white flesh and are more often enjoyed raw than cooked.

Pears

Citrus Fruits

Lemons and limes are interchangeable in most recipes, but lime has a more aromatic, intense flavor. Grapefruit may have green, yellow or pink-flushed skin, with yellow, green or pink flesh. Kumquats are tiny relatives of oranges and can be eaten whole, either raw or cooked. Oranges, satsumas, tangerines, clementines and numerous other small varieties of citrus fruits are virtually interchangeable.

Lemons

Oranges

Berries

The most popular are probably blackberries, blueberries, raspberries and strawberries. Do not overlook cranberries. Although too sharp to eat raw, their intense flavor and stunning color make them very good for cooking. Gooseberries used for cooking are small, firm, green and quite sharp, while other varieties are larger and sweeter.

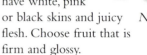

Strawberries

Pitted Fruits

Apricots, peaches, plums and nectarines may be used raw or lightly poached. White peaches have the sweetest flavor, and yellow varieties are more aromatic with a firmer texture. There are many dessert and cooking varieties of plums, ranging from pale gold to black. You can use slightly underripe plums for cooking. Sweet dessert cherries are available in the summer and have white, pink or black skins and juicy flesh. Choose fruit that is firm and glossy.

Nectarines

Exotic Fruits

Bananas are the most familiar exotic fruit, with a dense texture and sweet taste. Fresh dates are sweet and juicy and more succulent than dried. Cape

Dates

gooseberries are small, fragrant, pleasantly tart orange berries wrapped in a paper "cape." Fresh figs have green or purple skins and sweet, pinkish-red flesh. Available all year round, kiwi fruit need only peeling and slicing. Lychees are

Kiwi Fruit

small with hard pink skin and sweet-smelling, juicy flesh. The purplish brown skin of passion fruit is wrinkled when ripe. Cut the fruit in half and scoop out the juicy seeds. Pineapple, has juicy yellow flesh and is available all year. Star fruit falls into pretty five-pointed stars when sliced. The fruit is ripe when the

Passion Fruit

Star Fruit

Pineapples

edges begin to turn brown. The skins of mangoes vary in color, but the flesh should always be golden yellow, sweet and juicy. Papayas have smooth, yellow-orange skins when ripe. The flesh is orangey-pink and similar in texture to a melon. Pomegranate seeds and pulp have a delicate, slightly tart flavor.

Mangoes

Papayas

Melons, Figs & Grapes

There are many varieties of melons, from small sweet cantaloupes to large juicy red watermelons. Figs are delicious eaten fresh or dried. Red or green grapes are very popular for serving with cheese or in a fruit salad.

Watermelons

Fresh Figs

Grapes

Techniques

Peeling and Segmenting an Orange

1 Using a serrated knife, cut a thin slice from each end of the orange to expose the flesh. Cut off the peel, removing the white pith.

2 Hold the fruit over a bowl to catch the juice. Cut each segment between the membranes. Squeeze out the juice.

Peeling a Pineapple

1 Cut the pineapple across into slices of the desired thickness. Use a small, sharp knife to cut off the rind.

2 Hold each slice upright and cut out the "eyes." Remove the central core of each slice with an apple corer.

Preparing a Mango

1 Place the mango narrow-side down on a cutting board. Cut off a thick lengthwise slice, keeping the knife as close to the pit as possible. Turn the mango around and repeat on the other side. Cut off the flesh adhering to the pit and scoop out the flesh from the mango slices.

2 To make a "hedgehog," prepare the mango as above and score the flesh on each thick slice with criss-cross lines at ½-inch intervals, taking care not to cut through the skin.

3 Fold the mango halves inside out and serve.

4 When the mango is folded inside out, the cubes can be cut off using a sharp knife, if desired.

Freezing Berries

1 Open-freeze perfect specimens in a single layer on a baking sheet, then pack into rigid containers. Damaged berries can be puréed and sieved, then sweetened with sugar and frozen.

Peeling Pitted Fruits

These fruits, such as peaches, nectarines and apricots, can be peeled with a sharp paring knife, but this may waste some of the delicious flesh. The following method removes the skin only.

1 Make a tiny nick in the skin. Cover with boiling water and let sit for 15–30 seconds, depending on the ripeness of the fruit. Remove the fruit with a slotted spoon and peel off the skin, which should come off easily.

Removing Pits & Seeds

• To pit peaches, apricots etc., cut all around the fruit through the seam. Twist the halves in opposite directions, then lever out the pit with a knife.

• To pit cherries, put the fruit in a cherry pitter and push the bar into the fruit. The pit will be ejected.

• To remove grape seeds, cut the grapes in half, then pick out the seeds with the tip of a small sharp knife.

Cooked Fruit Purée

Fruit purées are a useful base for many desserts, and also make very good sauces for ice cream or tarts. They can be used immediately or left to cool and frozen for eating later.

1 Cook the fruit in a pan, with a small amount of water or sugar, until soft. If you use sugar alone, heat the fruit very gently, to prevent the sugar from burning, until the fruit juice begins to run and the sugar dissolves.

2 Remove any pits from the fruit and then transfer it to a food processor or blender and process until as smooth as desired. The mixture may then need to be sieved to achieve a velvety consistency.

Fresh Fruit with Mango Sauce

A salad made with fresh fruit is always refreshing and welcome but is especially delicious and attractive served with a puréed fruit sauce.

Serves 6

INGREDIENTS

1 large ripe mango, peeled, pitted
   and chopped
zest of 1 unwaxed orange
juice of 3 oranges
sugar, to taste
2 peaches
2 nectarines
1 small mango, peeled
2 plums
1 pear or ½ small melon
juice of 1 lemon
2 heaping tablespoons wild strawberries
   (optional)
2 heaping tablespoons raspberries
2 heaping tablespoons blueberries
small mint sprigs, to decorate

1 In a food processor fitted with the metal blade, process the mango until smooth. Add the orange zest, juice and sugar to taste and process again until very smooth. Press through a sieve into a bowl and chill the sauce.

2 Peel the peaches, if desired, then pit and slice the peaches, nectarines, mango and plums. Quarter the pear and remove the core or peel the melon, and slice thinly.

3 Place the sliced fruits on a large plate. Sprinkle with the lemon juice and chill, covered with plastic wrap, for up to 3 hours before serving. (Some fruits may discolor if cut too far ahead of time.)

4 To serve, arrange the sliced fruits on serving plates, spoon the berries on top, drizzle with a little mango sauce and decorate with mint sprigs. Serve the remaining sauce separately.

Fragrant Fruit Salad

The syrup of this exotic fruit salad is flavored and sweetened with lime and coffee liqueur. It can be prepared up to a day before serving.

Serves 6

INGREDIENTS
⅔ cup sugar
thinly pared zest and juice
   of 1 lime
¼ cup coffee liqueur, such as
   Tia Maria, Kahlúa or Toussaint
1 small pineapple
1 papaya
2 pomegranates
1 medium mango
2 passion fruits
fine strips of lime peel,
   to decorate

2 Using a sharp knife, cut the plume and stalk end from the pineapple. Peel thickly and cut the flesh into bite-size pieces, discarding the woody central core. Add to the bowl.

1 Put the sugar and lime zest in a small saucepan with ⅔ cup water. Heat gently until the sugar dissolves, then bring to a boil and simmer for 5 minutes. Let cool, then strain into a large serving bowl, discarding the lime zest. Stir in the lime juice and liqueur.

3 Cut the papaya in half and scoop out the seeds. Cut off the skin, then cut into chunks. Cut the pomegranates in half and scoop out the seeds. Break into clusters and add to the bowl.

4 Cut the mango lengthwise, along each side of the pit. Peel the skin off the flesh and cut into chunks. Add with the rest of the fruit to the bowl. Stir well.

5 Halve the passion fruits and scoop out the flesh using a teaspoon. Spoon onto the salad and serve, decorated with fine strips of lime peel.

COOK'S TIP: To maximize the flavor of the fruit, let the salad stand at room temperature for an hour before serving.

Strawberry & Avocado Salad in Ginger & Orange Sauce

Avocado is more often treated as a vegetable, but in the Caribbean it is used as a fruit, which of course it is!

Serves 4

INGREDIENTS
2 firm ripe avocados
3 firm ripe bananas, sliced
12 fresh strawberries, halved,
    or cherries
juice of 1 large orange
shredded fresh
    ginger root (optional)

FOR THE GINGER SYRUP
2 ounces fresh
    ginger root, chopped
3¾ cups water
1 cup sugar
2 cloves

2 Remove the ginger and discard. Let cool. Store in a covered container in the refrigerator.

3 Peel the avocados, cut into slices and place in a bowl with the bananas and strawberries or cherries.

COOK'S TIP: Avocados discolor when exposed to the air, so peel and slice them quickly. The orange juice and ginger syrup will prevent discoloration for some time.

1 First, make the ginger syrup; place the ginger, water, sugar and cloves in a saucepan and bring to a boil. Reduce the heat and simmer for about 1 hour, until well reduced and syrupy.

4 Pour the orange juice onto the fruits. Add ¼ cup of the ginger syrup and mix gently, using a metal spoon. Chill for 30 minutes and add a little shredded ginger, if desired.

Persian Melon

Called *Paludeh Garmac,* this is a typical Persian dessert using delicious, sweet fresh fruits flavored with rose water and a hint of aromatic mint.

Serves 4

INGREDIENTS
2 small melons
2 cups strawberries
3 peaches, peeled and cut into small cubes
1 bunch of seedless grapes (green or red)
2 tablespoons sugar
1 tablespoon rose water
1 tablespoon lemon juice
crushed ice (optional)
4 strawberries and sprigs of mint, to decorate

1 Cut the melons in half and remove the seeds. Scoop out the flesh with a melon baller, without damaging the skin. Reserve the melon shells. Alternatively, scoop out the flesh using a spoon and cut into bite-size pieces.

2 Reserve four strawberries and slice the others. Place in a bowl with the melon balls, the peaches, grapes, sugar, rose water and lemon juice.

3 Pile the fruit into the melon shells and chill in the refrigerator for 2 hours.

4 To serve, sprinkle with crushed ice, if desired, decorating each melon with a whole strawberry and a sprig of mint.

VARIATION: If preferred, nectarines and raspberries could replace the peaches and strawberries.

16

Fruits of the Tropics Salad

Pineapple, guavas, bananas and mango are combined with ginger and coconut to make this delectable Caribbean dessert.

Serves 4–6

INGREDIENTS
1 medium pineapple
14-ounce can guava halves
    in syrup
2 medium bananas, sliced
1 large mango, peeled, pitted
    and diced
4 ounces stem ginger and
    2 tablespoons of the syrup
¼ cup thick coconut milk
2 teaspoons sugar
½ teaspoon freshly
    grated nutmeg
½ teaspoon ground cinnamon
strips of coconut,
    to decorate

1 Peel, core and cube the pineapple, and place in a serving bowl. Drain the guavas, reserving the syrup, and chop. Add the guavas to the bowl with one of the bananas and the mango. Chop the stem ginger and add to the pineapple mixture.

2 Pour 2 tablespoons of the ginger syrup, and the reserved guava syrup into a blender or food processor and add the other banana, the coconut milk and the sugar. Process to make a smooth, creamy purée.

3 Pour the banana and coconut mixture onto the fruit; add a little nutmeg and cinnamon. Serve chilled, decorated with strips of coconut.

Fresh Fruit Salad

Any fruits in season can be used for this salad.

Serves 6

INGREDIENTS
2 apples
2 oranges
2 peaches
16–20 strawberries
2 tablespoons lemon juice
1–2 tablespoons orange flower water
confectioners' sugar, to taste
a few fresh mint leaves, to decorate

1 Peel, core and thinly slice the apples. Peel the oranges, removing all the pith, and segment them, catching any juice in a bowl.

2 Blanch the peaches for 1 minute in boiling water, then peel off the skin and cut the flesh into thick slices. Hull the strawberries and halve or quarter if large. Place all the fruit in a large serving bowl.

3 Blend together the lemon juice, orange flower water and any orange juice. Add a little confectioners' sugar, if desired. Pour the fruit juice mixture onto the fruit salad and serve decorated with mint leaves.

Right: Fresh Fruit Salad (top);
Dried Fruit Salad

Dried Fruit Salad

This is a wonderful combination of fresh and dried fruits.

Serves 4

INGREDIENTS
½ cup dried apricots
½ cup dried peaches
1 fresh pear
1 fresh apple
1 fresh orange
⅔ cup mixed raspberries
   and blackberries
1 cinnamon stick
¼ cup sugar
1 tablespoon honey
2 tablespoons lemon juice

1 Soak the apricots and peaches in water for 1–2 hours, until plump, then drain and halve or quarter them.

2 Peel and core the pear and apple and cut into cubes. Peel the orange with a sharp knife, removing all the pith, and cut into wedges. Place all the fruit in a saucepan with the berries.

3 Add 2½ cups water, the cinnamon, sugar and honey and bring to a boil. Cover and simmer very gently for 10–12 minutes, then remove the pan from heat. Stir in the lemon juice. Let cool, then pour into a serving bowl and chill for 1–2 hours before serving.

Blackberry Ice Cream

The sharpness of blackberries gives a delicious vibrancy to this superb and elegant ice cream. A delightful autumn dessert.

Serves 4–6

INGREDIENTS
5 cups blackberries, hulled,
   plus extra, to decorate
6 tablespoons sugar
2 tablespoons water
1¼ cups whipping cream
crisp cookies, to serve

1 Put the blackberries, sugar and water into a saucepan. Cover and simmer for 5 minutes, until the berries are just soft.

2 Transfer the fruit to a sieve placed over a bowl and press it through the mesh. Let cool, then chill.

3 If you are using an ice cream maker, churn the purée for 10–15 minutes, until it is thick, then gradually pour in the cream. Continue to churn until it is firm enough to scoop.

4 If you are making the ice cream by hand, whip the cream until it is just thick but still soft enough to fall from a spoon, then mix it with the chilled purée. Pour into a freezerproof container and freeze for 2 hours.

5 Mash the mixture with a fork, or beat with an electric mixer to break up the ice crystals. Return it to the freezer for 4 more hours, beating the mixture again after 2 hours. Scoop into dishes and decorate with blackberries. Serve with cookies.

Strawberry Semi Freddo

Serve this quick strawberry dessert semi-frozen to reap the full flavor. Crisp cookies make the perfect accompaniment.

Serves 4–6

INGREDIENTS
generous 2 cups strawberries
generous ½ cup strawberry jam
generous 1 cup ricotta cheese
scant 1 cup strained, plain yogurt
1 teaspoon vanilla extract
3 tablespoons sugar
extra strawberries and mint or lemon balm, to decorate

1 Put the strawberries in a bowl and mash them with a fork until broken into small pieces but not completely puréed. Stir in the jam.

2 Drain off any whey from the ricotta. Transfer it to a bowl and stir in the yogurt, vanilla and sugar.

3 Using a teaspoon, fold the mashed strawberries into the ricotta mixture until rippled.

4 Spoon into individual freezerproof dishes and freeze for at least 2 hours, until almost solid. Alternatively, freeze until completely solid, then transfer the ice cream to the refrigerator for about 45 minutes to soften before serving. Serve with extra strawberries and mint or lemon balm.

COOK'S TIPS: Don't mash the strawberries too much or they will liquefy. Freeze in a large container if you don't have suitable small dishes. Transfer to the refrigerator to thaw slightly, then scoop into glasses.

Peach & Cardamom Frozen Yogurt

This unusual peach frozen yogurt spiced with cardamom has a creamy, velvety texture.

Serves 4

INGREDIENTS

8 cardamom pods
6 peaches, total weight about 1¼ pounds, halved, and pitted
6 tablespoons sugar
2 tablespoons water
scant 1 cup plain yogurt

1 Put the cardamom pods on a board and crush them with the base of a ramekin, or use a mortar and pestle.

2 Chop the peaches roughly and put them in a saucepan. Add the crushed cardamom pods and seeds, the sugar and water. Cover and simmer for 10 minutes or until tender. Cool.

3 Transfer the peach mixture to a food processor or blender, process until smooth, then press through a sieve placed over a bowl. If you are using an ice cream maker, churn the purée until thick, then scrape it into a freezerproof container. Stir in the yogurt and freeze until firm enough to scoop.

4 If you are making the frozen yogurt by hand, sieve the peach purée into a bowl and stir in the yogurt. Pour the mixture into a plastic container and freeze for 5–6 hours, until firm, beating once or twice with a fork, electric mixer or in a food processor to break up the ice crystals. Scoop onto a large platter, or use a melon baller to make miniature scoops in individual dishes. Serve at immediately.

Mango & Orange Sorbet

Fresh and tangy, and gloriously vibrant in color, this sorbet is the perfect finale for a spicy meal.

Serves 2–4

INGREDIENTS
generous ½ cup brown sugar
2 large mangoes
juice of 1 orange
1 egg white (optional)
thinly pared strips of fresh
    unwaxed orange zest,
    to decorate

1 Gently heat the brown sugar and 1¼ cups water in a pan until the sugar has dissolved. Bring to a boil, then reduce the heat and simmer for 5 minutes. Let cool.

2 Cut off the two sides of the mango close to the pit. Peel, then cut the flesh off the pit. Dice the fruit. Process the mango flesh and orange juice in a food processor with the sugar syrup until smooth.

3 Pour the mixture into a freezerproof container and freeze for 2 hours, until semi-frozen. Whisk the egg white, if using, until it forms stiff peaks, then stir it into the sorbet. Whisk well to remove any ice crystals and freeze until solid.

4 Transfer the sorbet to the refrigerator 10 minutes before serving. Serve, decorated with orange zest.

Frozen Pear Terrine with Calvados & Chocolate Sauce

This terrine, based on a classic French dessert, is a refreshing and impressive end to any meal. For flavor, be sure the pears are fully ripe.

Serves 8

INGREDIENTS
3–3½ pounds ripe Williams pears
juice of 1 lemon
generous ½ cup sugar
10 whole cloves
6 tablespoons water
julienne strips of unwaxed orange zest,
    to decorate

FOR THE SAUCE
7 ounces semi-sweet chocolate
¼ cup hot strong black coffee
scant 1 cup heavy cream
2 tablespoons Calvados
    or brandy

2 Process the pears with their juice in a food processor or blender until smooth. Pour the purée into a freezerproof bowl, cover and freeze until firm.

3 Meanwhile, line a 2-pound loaf pan with plastic wrap. Let the plastic wrap overhang the sides. Spoon the frozen pear purée into a food processor or blender. Process until smooth. Pour into the prepared pan, cover and freeze until firm.

1 Peel, core and slice the pears. Place them in a saucepan with the lemon juice, sugar, cloves and water. Cover and simmer for 10 minutes. Remove the cloves. Let the pears cool.

4 Make the sauce. Break the chocolate into a large heatproof bowl set over a saucepan of hot water. When the chocolate has melted, stir in the coffee until smooth. Gradually stir in the cream and then the Calvados or brandy. Set the sauce aside.

5 About 20 minutes before serving, remove the pan from the freezer. Invert the terrine onto a plate, lift off the plastic wrap and place the terrine in the refrigerator to soften slightly. Warm the sauce over hot water. Place a slice of terrine on each dessert plate and spoon on some of the sauce. Decorate with julienne strips of orange zest and serve immediately.

Currant Apple Mousse

This Romanian recipe uses crisp apples and currants, macerated in red wine, to make a creamy mousse.

Serves 4–6

INGREDIENTS
¾ cup currants
¾ cup red wine,
    plus a little extra
4 apples, cored,
    peeled and sliced
1 cup water
generous 1 cup sugar
2 tablespoons cornstarch
few drops of pink food
    coloring (optional)
3 egg yolks
1 teaspoon vanilla extract
½ teaspoon cinnamon
2 egg whites
seedless red grapes, a little sugar and mint
    leaves to decorate

1 Soak the currants in the red wine for 1–1½ hours. Drain and set aside. Strain the wine through a fine sieve, then add more wine as necessary to make ¾ cup.

2 Meanwhile, put the apples in a pan and cook with the water and three-quarters of the sugar until soft. Cool, then process the apples in a food processor and return the purée to the pan.

3 Blend together the cornstarch and red wine and pour it into the purée. Cook for 8–10 minutes, stirring constantly. Add the food coloring, if using.

4 Beat the egg yolks in a bowl with the remaining sugar and the vanilla until pale and thick. Whisk the apple mixture slowly into the egg yolks. Add the cinnamon and beat until smooth.

5 Chill until thickened. Reserve 1 teaspoon of the egg white for decorating and whisk the remainder until stiff. Fold the currants and the whisked egg whites into the apple mixture, pour into glasses and chill.

6 Meanwhile, make the frosted grapes. Brush the red grapes with a little of the reserved egg white and sprinkle with sugar. Let dry. Use with the mint leaves to decorate the mousse, and serve.

Cold Mango Soufflés Topped with Toasted Coconut

Fragrant, fresh mango is one of the most delicious fruits around, whether it is simply served in slices or used as the basis for an ice cream or soufflé, as here.

Serves 4

INGREDIENTS
4 small mangoes, peeled, pitted
    and chopped
2 tablespoons water
1 tablespoon powdered gelatin
2 egg yolks
generous ½ cup sugar
½ cup milk
grated zest of 1 unwaxed orange
1¼ cups heavy cream
toasted flaked or coarsely shredded
    coconut, to decorate

1 Place a few pieces of mango in the bottom of each of four ⅔-cup ramekins. Wrap a greased collar of nonstick baking parchment around the outside of each dish, extending well above the rim. Secure with adhesive tape, then tie tightly with string.

2 Pour the water into a small heatproof bowl and sprinkle the powdered gelatin on the surface. Let sit for 5 minutes or until spongy. Place the bowl in a pan of hot water, stirring occasionally, until the gelatin has dissolved.

3 Meanwhile, whisk the egg yolks with the sugar and milk in another heatproof bowl. Place the bowl over a saucepan of simmering water and continue to whisk until the mixture is thick and frothy. Remove from heat and continue whisking until the mixture cools. Whisk in the liquid gelatin.

4 Process the remaining mango in a food processor or blender, then fold the purée into the egg yolk mixture with the orange zest. Set the mixture aside until starting to thicken.

5 Whip the heavy cream into soft peaks. Reserve 4 tablespoons and fold the rest into the mango mixture. Spoon into the ramekins until the mixture is 1 inch above the rim of each dish. Chill for 3–4 hours or until the mixture is set.

6 Carefully remove the paper collars from the soufflés. Spoon a little of the reserved cream on top of each soufflé and decorate with some toasted flaked or coarsely shredded coconut.

Orange-blossom Gelatin

This natural fruit gelatin has a cleansing quality that is welcome after a rich main course. Decorate it with edible flowers, if desired.

Serves 4–6

INGREDIENTS
5 tablespoons sugar
⅔ cup water
2 envelopes of powdered gelatin
  (about 1 ounce)
2½ cups freshly squeezed orange juice
2 tablespoons orange flower water

1 Place the sugar and water in a small saucepan and gently heat to dissolve the sugar, stirring occasionally. Let cool.

2 Sprinkle on the gelatin, ensuring that it is completely submerged in the water. Let stand until the gelatin has absorbed all the liquid and is solid.

3 Gently melt the gelatin over a bowl of simmering water until it becomes clear and transparent. Let cool. When the gelatin is cold, mix it with the orange juice and orange flower water.

4 Wet a mold and pour in the gelatin. Chill in the refrigerator for at least 2 hours or until set. Turn out to serve.

Apple Mint & Pink Grapefruit Fool

Besides looking particularly attractive, pink grapefruit is usually slightly less tart than the yellow varieties.

Serves 4–6

INGREDIENTS

1¼ pounds tart apples, peeled and sliced
8 ounces pink grapefruit segments
3 tablespoons honey
2 tablespoons water
6 large sprigs of apple mint,
   plus extra to decorate
⅔ cup heavy cream
1¼ cups custard

1 Place the apples, grapefruit, honey, water and apple mint in a pan, cover and simmer for 10 minutes, until soft.

2 Leave in the pan to cool, then discard the apple mint. Process the mixture in a food processor.

3 Whip the heavy cream until it forms soft peaks, and fold into the custard. Carefully fold the custard cream into the apple and grapefruit mixture, reserving 2 tablespoons to decorate.

4 Pour into individual glasses. Chill, then decorate with swirls of the remaining custard cream and small sprigs of apple mint.

Passion Fruit Crème Caramels with Dipped Cape Gooseberries

The aromatic flavor of passion fruit really permeates these delightful crème caramels. Cape Gooseberries are dipped in some of the caramel to create a unique decoration. These caramels will make an excellent dinner party dessert.

Serves 4

INGREDIENTS
scant 1 cup sugar
5 tablespoons water
4 passion fruits
4 cape gooseberries
3 eggs plus 1 egg yolk
⅔ cup heavy cream
⅔ cup creamy milk

2 Meanwhile, cut each passion fruit in half. Scoop out the seeds into a sieve set over a bowl. Press the seeds against the sieve to extract all their juice. Spoon a few of the seeds into each of four ⅔ cup ramekins. Set the juice aside.

1 Place ¾ cup of the sugar in a heavy saucepan. Add the water and heat gently until the sugar has dissolved. Increase the heat and boil until the syrup turns a dark golden color.

COOK'S TIP: Baking the custards in water stops them from curdling.

3 Peel off the papery casing from each cape gooseberry and dip the orange berries into the caramel. Place on a sheet of nonstick baking parchment and set aside. Pour the remaining caramel carefully into the ramekins.

4 Preheat the oven to 300°F. Whisk the eggs, egg yolk and remaining sugar in a bowl. Whisk in the cream and milk, then the passion fruit juice. Strain into each ramekin, then place the ramekins in a baking pan. Pour in hot water to come halfway up the sides of the dishes and bake for 40–45 minutes or until just set.

5 Remove the custards from the pan and let cool, then cover and chill them for 4 hours before serving. Run a knife between the edge of each ramekin and the custard and invert each in turn onto a dessert plate. Shake the ramekins firmly to release the custards. Decorate each with a dipped cape gooseberry.

Jamaican Fruit Trifle

A deliciously light version of a traditional Caribbean dessert contains plenty of fruit and is made with crème fraîche, as well as cream.

Serves 8

INGREDIENTS
1 large sweet pineapple, peeled and cored, about 12 ounces, leaves reserved
1¼ cups heavy cream
scant 1 cup crème fraîche
¼ cup confectioners' sugar, sifted
2 teaspoons vanilla extract
2 tablespoons white or coconut rum
3 papayas, peeled, seeded and chopped
3 mangoes, peeled, pitted and chopped
thinly pared zest and juice of 1 lime
⅓ cup coarsely shredded or flaked coconut, toasted, (optional)

1 Cut the pineapple into large chunks, place in a food processor or blender and process briefly until chopped. Transfer to a sieve placed over a bowl and let sit for 5 minutes so that most of the juice drains off the fruit.

COOK'S TIP: It is important to let the chopped pineapple drain thoroughly, otherwise the pineapple cream will be watery. Don't throw away the drained pineapple juice—mix it with seltzer water for a refreshing drink.

2 Whip the heavy cream to very soft peaks, then lightly but thoroughly fold in the crème fraîche, sifted confectioners' sugar, vanilla and rum.

3 Fold the drained, chopped pineapple into the cream mixture. Place the chopped papayas and mangoes in a large bowl and pour in the lime juice. Gently stir the fruit mixture to combine. Shred the pared lime zest.

4 Divide the fruit mixture and the pineapple cream among eight dessert plates. Decorate with the lime shreds, toasted coconut, if using, and small pineapple leaves, and serve immediately.

Apricot & Hazelnut Meringue Roll with Apricot Brandy

A soft nutty meringue, rolled around a creamy apricot filling spiked with apricot brandy, is a superb dinner party dessert.

Serves 6

INGREDIENTS
5 egg whites
¾ cup sugar
1 teaspoon cornstarch
½ cup toasted hazelnuts, chopped
confectioners' sugar, for dusting
apricot slices and mint sprigs,
    to decorate

FOR THE FILLING
1¼ cups heavy cream
2 tablespoons apricot brandy
¼ cup apricot conserve, any large
    chunks chopped
6 apricots, pitted and thinly sliced

1 Preheat the oven to 225°F. Grease a 12 x 8-inch jelly roll pan and line it with nonstick baking parchment. Whisk the egg whites until stiff but not dry. Whisk in half the sugar and then continue to whisk until the mixture is stiff. Fold in the remaining sugar.

VARIATION: You can add extra texture and flavor by turning the baked meringue onto a sheet of nonstick baking parchment dusted with ground hazelnuts.

2 Fold in the cornstarch and hazelnuts and spoon the mixture into the pan. Bake for about 45 minutes or until set. Leave the meringue in the pan to cool, uncovered, for 1 hour.

3 Whip the cream lightly in a bowl, then stir in the apricot brandy and conserve. Fold in the apricot slices.

4 Dust a sheet of nonstick baking parchment with confectioners' sugar and turn the meringue onto it. Peel off the lining paper and spread the filling on top of the meringue.

5 With the aid of the parchment, and working from a short end, roll the meringue over the filling. Place the roll on a serving plate, dust with more confectioners' sugar and decorate with apricot slices and mint sprigs.

Raspberry Millefeuille

Succulent raspberries and luscious confectioner's custard are sandwiched between layers of melt-in-your-mouth puff pastry.

Serves 8

INGREDIENTS
1 pound puff pastry, thawed if frozen
6 egg yolks
⅓ cup sugar
3 tablespoons all-purpose flour
1½ cups milk
2 tablespoons kirsch or cherry liqueur (optional)
2⅔ cups raspberries
confectioners' sugar, for dusting
strawberry or raspberry *coulis,* to serve

1 Lightly butter two large baking sheets and sprinkle them very lightly with cold water.

2 On a lightly floured surface, roll out the pastry to a ⅛-inch thickness. Using a 4-inch cutter, cut out 12 rounds. Place on the baking sheets and prick each a few times with a fork. Chill for 30 minutes. Preheat the oven to 400°F.

3 Bake the pastry rounds for 15–20 minutes, until golden, then transfer to wire racks to cool.

4 Whisk the egg yolks and sugar for 2 minutes, until light and creamy, then whisk in the flour until just blended. Bring the milk to a boil over medium heat and pour it over the egg mixture, whisking to blend.

5 Return to the saucepan, bring to a boil and boil for 2 minutes, whisking constantly. Remove the pan from heat and whisk in the kirsch or liqueur, if using. Pour into a bowl and press plastic wrap on the surface to prevent a skin from forming. Set aside to cool.

COOK'S TIP: To make a raspberry or strawberry *coulis,* crush 1¼ cups berries into a purée with a fork, then rub through a fine strainer set over a clean bowl with the back of a spoon. Sweeten with confectioners' sugar.

6 Carefully split the pastry rounds in half. Spread one round at a time with a little custard. Arrange a layer of raspberries on the custard and top with a second pastry round. Spread with a little more custard and a few more raspberries. Top with a third pastry round flat-side up. Dust with confectioners' sugar and serve with the *coulis*.

Coffee Pavlova with Tropical Fruits

You can use virtually any fruit in season to decorate the meringue base—let your imagination run wild.

Serves 6–8

INGREDIENTS
2 tablespoons ground coffee, e.g. mocha
2 tablespoons near-boiling water
3 egg whites
½ teaspoon cream of tartar
scant 1 cup sugar
1 teaspoon cornstarch, sifted

FOR THE FILLING
⅔ cup heavy cream
1 teaspoon orange flower water
⅔ cup crème fraîche
1¼ pounds sliced tropical fruits, such as mango, papaya and kiwi
1 tablespoon confectioners' sugar, (optional)

2 Put the coffee in a small bowl and pour in the hot water. Let infuse for 4 minutes, then strain through a very fine sieve.

3 Whisk the egg whites with the cream of tartar until stiff, but not dry. Gradually whisk in the sugar until the meringue is stiff and shiny, then quickly whisk in the cornstarch and coffee.

4 Using a long knife or spatula, spread the meringue mixture onto the prepared baking sheet into an even 8-inch round. Make a slight hollow in the middle. Bake for 1 hour, then turn off the heat and leave in the oven until cool.

1 Preheat the oven to 275°F. Draw an 8-inch circle on nonstick baking parchment. Place pencil-side down on a baking sheet.

VARIATION: 1 pound berries, such as wild or cultivated strawberries, raspberries or blueberries, may be used instead of the tropical fruits.

5 Peel off the lining paper and transfer the meringue to a serving plate. To make the filling, whip the heavy cream with the orange flower water until soft peaks form. Fold in the crème fraîche. Spoon into the center of the meringue. Arrange the tropical fruits on the cream and dust with confectioners' sugar, if using.

Bananas with Lime & Cardamom Sauce

These delicious spiced bananas can also be served with folded crêpes.

Serves 6

INGREDIENTS
6 bananas
¼ cup butter
seeds from 4 cardamom pods, crushed
½ cup sliced almonds
thinly pared zest and juice of 2 limes
¼ cup light brown sugar
2 tablespoons dark rum
vanilla ice cream, to serve

1 Peel the bananas and cut them in half lengthwise. Heat half the butter in a large frying pan. Add half the bananas, and cook until the undersides are golden. Turn carefully, using a spatula. Cook until golden.

2 As they cook, transfer the bananas to a heatproof serving dish. Cook the remaining bananas in the same way.

3 Melt the remaining butter, then add the cardamom seeds and almonds. Cook, stirring, until golden.

4 Stir in the lime zest and juice, then the sugar. Cook, stirring, until the mixture is smooth, bubbling and slightly reduced. Stir in the rum. Pour the sauce onto the bananas and serve immediately, with vanilla ice cream.

VARIATION: If you prefer not to use alcohol in your cooking, replace the rum with fresh fruit juice.

Citrus Fruit Flambé with Pistachio Praline

Serves 4

INGREDIENTS
oil, for greasing
generous ½ cup sugar
½ cup pistachios
4 oranges
2 ruby grapefruit
2 limes
¼ cup butter
¼ cup light brown sugar
3 tablespoons Cointreau
fresh mint sprigs, to decorate

1 Brush a baking sheet with oil. Place the sugar and nuts in a heavy saucepan and cook gently, swirling the pan, until the sugar has melted. Cook over low heat until the nuts start to pop and the sugar has turned dark gold.

2 Pour onto the baking sheet and cool. Chop the praline into chunks.

3 Cut off the zest and pith from the citrus fruit. Cut between the membranes so that the segments fall into a bowl, with any juice.

4 Heat the butter and sugar in a heavy frying pan until the sugar has melted. Strain the citrus juices into the pan and cook, stirring occasionally, until reduced and syrupy.

5 Add the fruit segments and warm through without stirring. Pour on the Cointreau and set it on fire. When the flames die down, spoon the flambé into serving dishes. Serve sprinkled with praline and decorated with mint.

Apple Soufflé Omelette

This delicious autumn filling is made by sautéing apples until they are slightly caramelized — you could use fresh berries in the summer.

Serves 2

INGREDIENTS
4 eggs, separated
2 tablespoons light cream
1 tablespoon caster sugar
1 tablespoon butter
confectioners' sugar, for dredging

FOR THE FILLING
1 apple, peeled, cored and sliced
2 tablespoons butter
2 tablespoons light brown sugar
3 tablespoons light cream

1 To make the filling, sauté the apple slices in the butter and sugar in a heavy pan over low heat until just tender. Stir in the cream and keep warm, while making the omelet.

COOK'S TIP: When whisking egg whites, make sure that the bowl and whisk are both greasefree and that there is no yolk mixed in.

2 Place the egg yolks in a bowl with the cream and sugar and beat well. Whisk the egg whites until stiff, then fold into the yolk mixture using a figure-eight motion.

3 Melt the butter in a large, heavy frying pan, and pour in the soufflé mixture evenly. Cook for 1 minute, until golden underneath, then place under a hot broiler to brown the top.

4 Slide the omelet onto a plate, add the apple mixture, then fold over. Sift the confectioners' sugar on thickly, then mark in a criss-cross pattern with a hot metal skewer. Serve immediately.

Peach & Raspberry Crumble

A quick and easy dessert, this crumble is good served hot or cold, on its own, or with custard.

Serves 4

INGREDIENTS
⅔ cup whole-wheat flour
¾ cup medium oatmeal
6 tablespoons butter
¼ cup light brown sugar
½ teaspoon ground cinnamon
14-ounce can peach slices in juice
1⅓ cups raspberries
2 tablespoons honey
sprig of fresh mint, to garnish

1 Preheat the oven to 350°F. Put the flour and oatmeal in a bowl and combine.

2 Rub in the butter until the mixture resembles bread crumbs, then stir in the sugar and cinnamon.

3 Drain the peach slices and reserve the juice. Chop the peach slices to about the same size as the raspberries.

4 Arrange the chopped peaches evenly on the bottom of an ovenproof dish, then sprinkle on the raspberries.

5 Combine the reserved peach juice and honey, pour the mixture onto the fruit and stir.

VARIATION: For a tasty change, use other combinations of fruit, such as apples and blackberries, rhubarb and orange, or strawberries and pineapple. If using all fresh fruit, add a little fruit juice.

6 Spoon the crumble mixture onto the fruit, pressing it down lightly. Bake for about 45 minutes, until golden brown on top. Garnish with fresh mint and serve hot or cold.

Apricot Panettone Bread Pudding

Slices of light-textured panettone are layered with dried apricots and cooked in a creamy coffee custard for a satisfyingly warming dessert.

Serves 4

INGREDIENTS
4 tablespoons unsalted butter, softened
½-inch thick slices (about 14 ounces)
    panettone containing candied fruit
¾ cup dried apricots, chopped
1⅔ cups milk
1 cup heavy cream
¼ cup mild-flavored
    ground coffee
½ cup sugar
3 eggs
2 tablespoons brown sugar
cream or crème fraîche,
    to serve

2 Pour the milk and cream into a pan and heat until almost boiling. Pour the milk mixture onto the coffee and let infuse for 10 minutes. Strain through a fine sieve, discarding the coffee grounds.

3 Lightly beat the sugar and eggs together, then whisk in the warm coffee-flavored milk. Slowly pour the mixture on the panettone. Let soak for 15 minutes.

4 Sprinkle the top of the bread pudding with brown sugar and place the dish in a large roasting pan. Pour in enough boiling water to come halfway up the sides of the dish.

1 Preheat the oven to 325°F. Brush an 8-cup oval ovenproof dish with 1 tablespoon of the butter. Spread the panettone with the remaining butter and arrange in the dish. Cut to fit, and sprinkle the apricots among and on top of the layers.

5 Bake for 40–45 minutes, until the top is golden and crusty, but the middle still slightly wobbly. Remove from the oven, but leave the dish in the hot water for 10 minutes. Serve warm with cream or crème fraîche.

Coffee Crêpes with Peaches & Cream

Juicy golden peaches and cream conjure up the sweet taste of summer. Here, they are delicious, as the filling for these light coffee crêpes.

Serves 6

INGREDIENTS
⅔ cup all-purpose flour
¼ cup buckwheat flour
¼ teaspoon salt
1 egg, beaten
scant 1 cup milk
1 tablespoon butter, melted
scant ½ cup strong brewed coffee, strained
sunflower oil, for frying

FOR THE FILLING
6 ripe peaches
1¼ cups heavy cream
1 tablespoon amaretto liqueur
1 cup mascarpone cheese
5 tablespoons sugar
2 tablespoons confectioners'
    sugar, for dusting (optional)

1 Sift the flours and salt into a mixing bowl. Make a well in the middle and add the egg, half the milk and the melted butter. Gradually mix in the flour, beating until smooth, then beat in the remaining milk and coffee.

COOK'S TIP: To keep the crêpes warm while you make the rest, cover them with foil and place the plate over a pan of barely simmering water.

2 Heat a drizzle of oil in a 6–8-inch crêpe pan. Pour in just enough batter to cover the bottom of the pan. Cook for 2–3 minutes, until the underneath is golden brown, then flip over and cook the other side.

3 Slide the crêpe out of the pan onto a plate. Continue making crêpes in this way until all the mixture is used, stacking and interleaving with waxed paper.

4 To make the filling, halve the peaches and remove the pits. Cut into thick slices. Whip the cream and amaretto liqueur until soft peaks form. Beat the mascarpone with the sugar until smooth. Beat 2 tablespoons of the cream into the mascarpone, then fold in the remainder.

5 Spoon a little of the amaretto cream onto one half of each pancake and top with peach slices. Gently fold the pancake over and dust with confectioners' sugar, if desired. Serve immediately.

Fresh Fig Phyllo Tart

Figs cook wonderfully well and taste superb in this tart—the riper the figs, the better they will taste.

Serves 6–8

INGREDIENTS
five 14 x 10-inch sheets phyllo pastry,
    thawed if frozen
2 tablespoons butter, melted, plus extra,
    for greasing
6 fresh figs, cut into wedges
⅔ cup all-purpose flour
6 tablespoons sugar
4 eggs
scant 2 cups creamy milk
½ teaspoon almond extract
1 tablespoon confectioners' sugar,
    for dusting
whipped cream or plain yogurt, to serve

1 Preheat the oven to 375°F. Grease a 10 x 6¼-inch baking pan with butter. Brush each phyllo sheet in turn with melted butter and use to line the prepared pan.

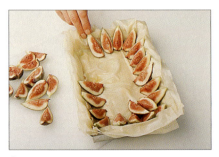

2 Using scissors, cut off any excess pastry, leaving a little overhanging the edge. Arrange the figs in the phyllo case.

3 Sift the flour into a bowl and stir in the sugar. Add the eggs and a little of the milk and whisk until smooth. Gradually whisk in the remaining milk and the almond extract. Pour the mixture onto the figs and bake for 1 hour or until the batter has set and is golden.

4 Remove the tart from the oven and let cool in the pan on a wire rack for 10 minutes. Remove from the pan, if desired. Dust with the confectioners' sugar and serve with whipped cream or plain yogurt.

Exotic Fruit Tranche

This is a good way to make the most of a small selection of tropical fruit and looks simply amazing.

Serves 8

INGREDIENTS
1½ cups all-purpose flour
¼ cup unsalted butter
2 tablespoons vegetable shortening
¼ cup sugar
2 egg yolks
about 1 tablespoon cold water
scant ½ cup apricot conserve, sieved and warmed

FOR THE FILLING
⅔ cup heavy cream,
 plus extra to serve
generous 1 cup mascarpone cheese
¼ cup confectioners' sugar, sifted
grated zest of 1 unwaxed orange
3 cups mixed prepared fruits,
 such as mango, papaya, star fruit,
 kiwi fruit and blackberries
6 tablespoons apricot conserve, sieved
 and 1 tablespoon white or coconut
 rum, to glaze

1 Sift the flour into a bowl and rub in the butter and vegetable shortening until the mixture resembles fine bread crumbs. Stir in the sugar. Add the egg yolks and enough cold water to make a soft dough.

2 Thinly roll out the pastry between two sheets of plastic wrap and use to line a 14 x 4½-inch fluted tranche pan. Let the excess pastry hang over the edge of the pan and chill for 30 minutes.

3 Preheat the oven to 400°F. Prick the bottom of the pastry shell with a fork, and line with nonstick baking parchment and baking beans. Bake for 10–12 minutes.

4 Lift out the paper and beans and return the pastry to the oven for 5 minutes. Trim off the excess pastry and brush the inside with the warmed apricot conserve to form a seal. Let cool on a wire rack.

5 Make the filling. Whip the heavy cream into soft peaks, then stir it into the mascarpone with the confectioners' sugar and orange zest. Spread the mixture inside the cooled pastry shell and top with the prepared fruits.

6 Warm the remaining apricot conserve with the rum, and drizzle or brush on the fruits to make a glaze. Serve the tranche with extra cream.

VARIATION: If you don't have a tranche pan, line a 9-inch tart pan with the pastry.

Pear & Blueberry Pie

Bursting with fruit and full of flavor, this double-crust pie is the perfect choice for a family supper.

Serves 4

INGREDIENTS
2 cups all-purpose flour
pinch of salt
¼ cup lard, cubed
¼ cup butter, cubed
5 cups blueberries
2 tablespoons sugar
1 tablespoon arrowroot
2 ripe, but firm, pears, peeled,
    cored and sliced
½ teaspoon ground cinnamon
grated zest of ½ unwaxed lemon
beaten egg, to glaze
sugar, for sprinkling
crème fraîche, to serve

1 Sift the flour and salt into a bowl and rub in the lard and butter until the mixture resembles fine bread crumbs. Stir in 3 tablespoons cold water and mix into a dough. Chill for 30 minutes.

2 Place 2 cups of the blueberries in a pan with the sugar. Cover and cook gently until the blueberries have softened. Press through a nylon sieve to remove the seeds.

3 Blend the arrowroot with 2 tablespoons cold water and add to the blueberry purée. Bring to a boil, stirring until thickened. Cool slightly.

4 Place a baking sheet in the oven and preheat to 375°F. Roll out just over half the pastry on a lightly floured surface and use to line an 8-inch shallow pie pan.

5 Combine the remaining blueberries, the pears, cinnamon and lemon rind and spoon into the dish. Pour the blueberry purée on top.

6 Roll out the remaining pastry and use to cover the pie. Make a small slit in the center. Brush with egg and sprinkle with sugar. Bake the pie on the hot baking sheet for 40–45 minutes, until golden. Serve warm with crème fraîche.

Fresh Lemon Tart

This refreshing tart should be served at room temperature if the zesty lemon flavor is to be enjoyed to the fullest.

Serves 6–8

INGREDIENTS
12 ounces ready-made rich sweet shortcrust pastry, thawed if frozen

FOR THE FILLING
3 eggs
generous ½ cup sugar
1 cup ground almonds
7 tablespoons heavy cream
grated zest and juice of
    2 unwaxed lemons

FOR THE TOPPING
2 thin-skinned unwaxed lemons,
    thinly sliced
1 cup sugar
7 tablespoons water

1 Roll out the pastry and use it to line a deep 9-inch fluted tart pan. Prick the base with a fork and chill for 30 minutes.

2 Preheat the oven to 400°F. Line the pastry with nonstick baking parchment and baking beans and bake blind for 10 minutes. Remove the paper and beans and return the pastry to the oven for 5 more minutes.

3 Meanwhile, make the filling. Beat the eggs, sugar, almonds and cream in a bowl until smooth. Beat in the lemon zest and juice. Pour the filling into the pastry. Lower the oven temperature to 375°F and bake for 20 minutes or until the filling has set and the pastry is lightly golden.

4 Make the topping. Place the lemon slices in a pan and pour in water to cover. Simmer for 15–20 minutes or until the skins are tender, then drain.

VARIATION: If you prefer not to candy the lemons, simply dust the tart with confectioners' sugar.

5 Place the sugar in a saucepan and stir in the measured water. Heat gently until the sugar has dissolved, stirring constantly, then boil for 2 minutes. Add the lemon slices and cook for 10–15 minutes, until the skins become shiny and candied.

6 Lift out the candied lemon slices and arrange them on top of the tart. Return the syrup to the heat and boil until reduced to a thick glaze. Brush this on the tart and let cool completely before serving, but do not chill.

Cherry Strudel

While quite time-consuming to make, cherry strudel, with its light-as-air texture and fruity filling, is well worth the effort.

Serves 8–10

INGREDIENTS
scant 3 cups all-purpose flour
1 egg, beaten
10 tablespoons butter, melted
scant ½ cup warm water
sifted confectioners' sugar, for dredging

FOR THE FILLING
generous ½ cup walnuts,
    roughly chopped
generous ½ cup sugar
1½ pounds cherries, pitted
¾ cup day-old
    bread crumbs

1 Preheat the oven to 400°F. Put the flour in a warm bowl. Make a well in the center, add the egg, ½ cup of the melted butter and the water. Mix into a smooth, pliable dough, adding a little extra flour if needed. Leave wrapped in plastic wrap for 30 minutes to rest.

2 Meanwhile, in a large bowl, combine the chopped walnuts, sugar, cherries and bread crumbs.

3 Lay out a clean dish towel and sprinkle it with flour. Carefully roll out the dough until it covers the towel. The dough should be as thin as possible, so that you can see the design on the cloth through it.

4 Dampen the edges with water. Spread the cherry filling on the pastry, leaving a gap all the way around the edge, about 1 inch wide. Roll up the pastry carefully with the side edges folded in over the filling to prevent it from coming out. Use the dish towel to help you roll the pastry.

5 Brush the strudel with the remaining melted butter. Place on a baking sheet and curl into a horseshoe shape. Cook for 30–40 minutes or until golden brown. Dredge with confectioners' sugar and serve warm or cold.

Upside-down Apple Tart

A special *tarte tatin*—the original French name of this dish—pan is ideal, but an ovenproof frying pan will do very well.

Serves 8–10

INGREDIENTS
8 ounces puff or shortcrust pastry,
    thawed if frozen
10–12 large Golden Delicious apples
lemon juice
½ cup butter, cut into pieces
generous ½ cup sugar
½ teaspoon ground cinnamon
crème fraîche or whipped cream,
    to serve

1 On a lightly floured surface, roll out the pastry into an 11-inch round less than ¼-inch thick. Transfer to a lightly floured baking sheet and chill.

2 Peel the apples, cut them in half lengthwise and core. Sprinkle the apples generously with lemon juice.

3 In a 10-inch *tarte tatin* pan, cook the butter, sugar and cinnamon over medium heat until the butter has melted and the sugar has dissolved, stirring occasionally.

4 Continue cooking for 6–8 minutes, until the mixture turns a medium caramel color, then remove the pan from heat and arrange the apple halves, standing on their edges, in the pan, packing them in tightly since they shrink during cooking.

5 Return the apple-filled pan to the heat and bring to a simmer over medium heat for 20–25 minutes, until the apples are tender and colored. Remove the pan from heat and cool slightly.

6 Preheat the oven to 450°F. Place the pastry on top of the apple-filled pan and tuck the edges of the pastry inside the edge of the pan around the apples. Pierce the pastry in two or three places, then bake for 25–30 minutes, until the pastry is golden and the filling is bubbling. Let cool in the pan for 10–15 minutes.

7 To serve, run a sharp knife around edge of the pan to loosen the pastry. Cover with a serving plate and, holding them tightly, carefully invert the pan and plate together (do this carefully, preferably over the sink in case any caramel drips). Lift up the pan and loosen any apples that stick with a rounded knife. Serve warm with cream.

This edition is published by Southwater

Distributed in the UK by
The Manning Partnership,
251–253 London Road East, Batheaston,
Bath BA1 7RL, UK
tel. (0044) 01225 852 727
fax. (0044) 01225 852 852

Distributed in Australia by
Sandstone Publishing,
Unit 1, 360 Norton Street, Leichhardt,
New South Wales 2040, Australia
tel. (0061) 2 9560 7888
fax. (0061) 2 9560 7488

Distributed in New Zealand by
Five Mile Press NZ,
PO Box 33–1071, Takapuna,
Auckland 9, New Zealand
tel. (0064) 9 4444 144
fax. (0064) 9 4444 518

Southwater is an imprint of Anness Publishing Limited

© 2000 Anness Publishing Limited

Publisher: Joanna Lorenz
Editor: Valerie Ferguson
Series Designer: Bobbie Colgate Stone
Designer: Andrew Heath
Editorial Reader: Marion Wilson
Production Controller: Joanna King

Recipes contributed by: Catherine Atkinson, Carole Clements, Trisha Davies, Nicola Diggins, Joanna
Farrow, Shirley Gill, Rosamund Grant, Sarah Lewis, Maggie Mayhew, Norma Miller, Katherine
Richmond, Anne Sheasby, Liz Trigg, Elizabeth Wolf-Cohen.

Photography: Karl Adamson,
William Adams-Lingwood, Louise Dare,
John Freeman, Michelle Garrett, Ian Garlick, Amanda Heywood, Janine Hosegood,
David Jordan, Patrick McLeavey, Thomas Odulate.

1 3 5 7 9 10 8 6 4 2